RANDOM ACTS OF DRAW-NESS!

→ BY BRADY SMITH

Penguin Workshop

W

PENGUIN WORKSHOP
An Imprint of Penguin Random House LLC, New York

Visit us online at www.penguinrandomhouse.com.

ISBN 9780593384053   10 9 8 7 6 5 4 3 2 1

This book is for
Harper, Holt, Pace, Brae, Olivia, Will,
Gus, Zoe, Isaac, Graycen, Valerie, Mia,
Cleary, Joseph, Emily, Jake, Gordon,
Natalia, Lincoln, Bianca, Bailey, Ava,
Scarlett, Nico, GiGi, Brooklyn, Grace,
Avery, Dante, Hayden, Kelsey, Ethan,
Ruby, Liam, Lauren, Jeff, Lisa, Lukas,
Finton, Mary, Xayden, Angela, Izzy, Luca,
Kathy, Ben, Jonah, Avery, The Easter
Bunny, Dash, Tamara, Annabelle, Brooke,
Saylor, Georgia, Scout, Nick, Noah, Nolan,
Redford, Caroline, Tiffani, Oliver, Pam,
Anna, Taylor, Camille, Wyatt, Douglas,
Jimmy, Julian, Roseanne, Reve, Whitney,
Shane, Brianna, Sarah, Claire, Evelyn,
Sophia, Leah, MiMi, Braelyn, Bella, Peggy,
Lottie, Benjamin, Clara, Ramini, Ellie,
Shaun, Elisa, Kaden, Aaron, Aubrey, Ryley,
Arianna, Sam, Lori, Shawna, Ilsa, Noelle,
Chuck, Karen, Tyler, and everyone else
who sent in a drawing challenge!

INTRODUCTION

Wooohoooo!! The official *Random Acts of Drawness!* book! Possibly the most epic, awesome, super-duper, silly, hilarious coloring/activity book in the history of the world is in YOUR HANDS at this precise moment in time! Cool, right?

You may be asking, how did this happen? Back in March 2020, when lockdown was just beginning, I had an idea. What if I posted a daily video of a thirty-second drawing challenge on my Instagram feed for people and families, like my own, who were stuck at home?

So, I set up my camera, drew the first challenge, and posted it that very day. Before I knew it, I was receiving drawing requests from kids and families all over the world! After one hundred days and one hundred drawings, the video challenges came to an end . . . but this book was born! And I couldn't have done it without everyone who sent in all their amazing, random ideas.

As you go through this book, I have a few things to ask: Draw fast! Draw sloppy! Color outside the lines! Be silly! And most importantly, HAVE FUN! I hope this book unleashes a creativity in you that you didn't even know was there, and brings you a whole bunch of joy.

—Brady Smith

When you see this logo in the book, draw the prompt in thirty seconds!

RANDOM ACTS OF DRAW-NESS!

Time to get super creative super fast!

Here's an example:
Boy riding a cheeseburger with wings.

Try tracing
it here!

Here's
that
logo!

RaNDOM ACTS of DRAW-NeSS!

THUMBS UP!

Okay. Grab a marker
(not permanent, please) and color
your thumb. Now . . . press your
thumb down on the page, and then
turn that smudge into a creature.
Cool. Now, make a story using your
thumbprint characters at each of
the locations listed below.

A city, an ocean floor, a
playground, and a prehistoric
pasture all need to be populated.

Like
this!

Flip to page 44 if you want to
work on more thumbprints.

A dog eating ice cream and walking a person.

Here's an example.

RaNDoM AcTs oF DRAW-Ness!

A koala eating a
french fry/banana sandwich.

The Queen having tea
with an octopus.

Art can start from anywhere and anything—even from an itty-bitty line. So take a crack at some:

Try it out using the prompts, starting on the next page.

Using this line, draw a robot watering a tree that's growing cupcakes.

Take this line and turn it into a
dinosaur dressed as a cowboy.

Take this line and turn it into
a sloth playing tennis.

Very good drawing so far! Now, draw a panda bear driving a car with a UFO parked on the roof. Oh, and put an alien waiting inside the UFO.

Now make this line into a rhinoceros riding in a rocket ship.

Flip to page 60 if you want to work on more line art!

A superhero chihuahua rescuing someone from a man-eating cheeseburger.

Grab a pen (or crayon, whatever)
and put the tip at the paper's edge.
Now, close your eyes and draw a line.
Can you hit the bull's-eye?

Move the pen to a new place
on the paper and try again.
Remember, eyes closed! You got this!

On these couple pages . . .
invent new shapes!

Like a box and triangle . . . BOANGLE!
Maybe a circle and a square . . . SQUIRCLE!
Most importantly, just draw and have fun!

Scribble on these pages while you count to 100!

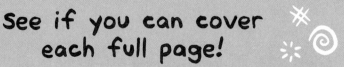

See if you can cover
each full page!

you got
this!

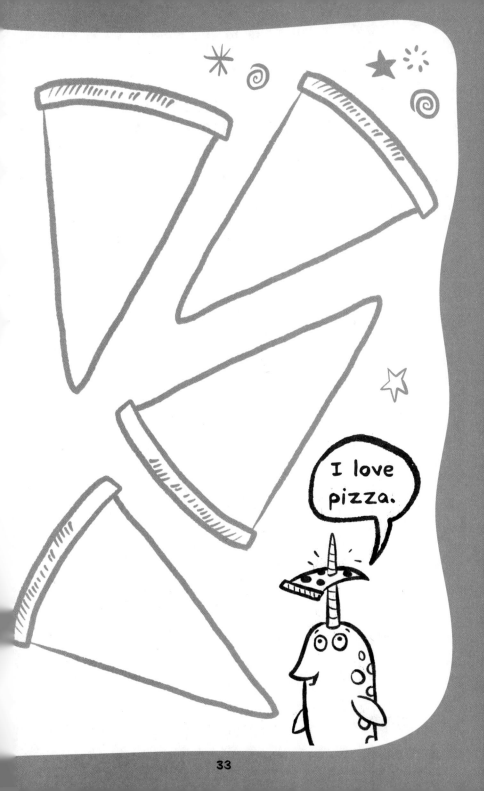

A man riding a horse in the water and holding a monster eating a cake.

A unicorn and a shark flying
hearts over the world.

Draw Your Own Comic!

(Need help with characters? Go to page 39.)

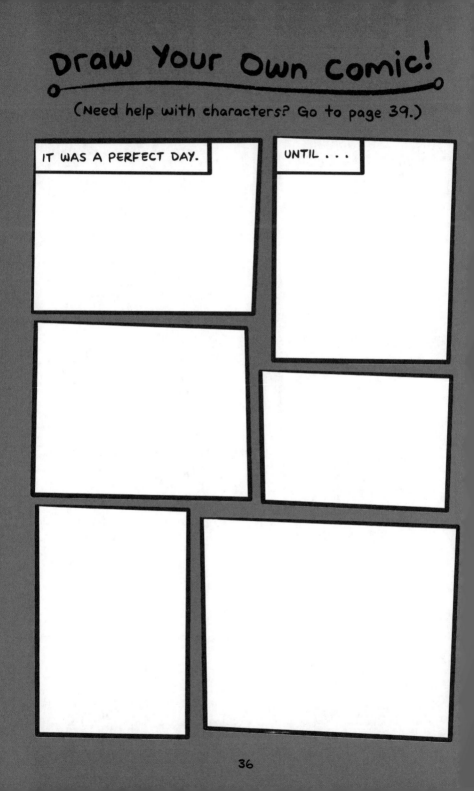

IT WAS A PERFECT DAY.

UNTIL . . .

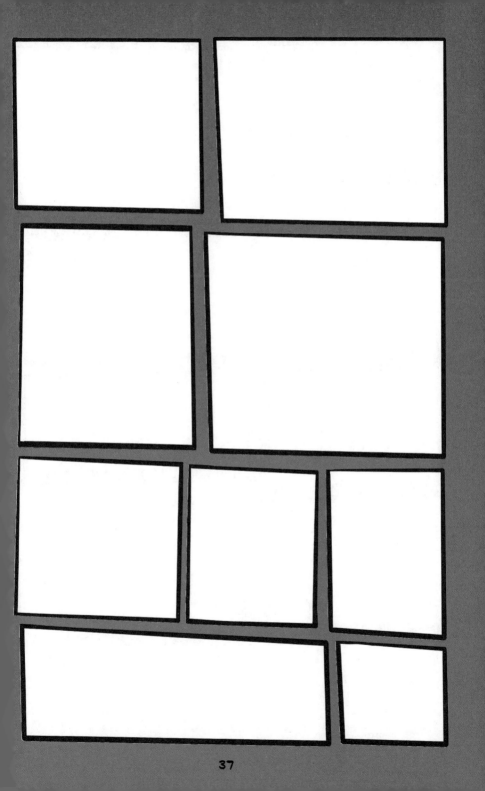

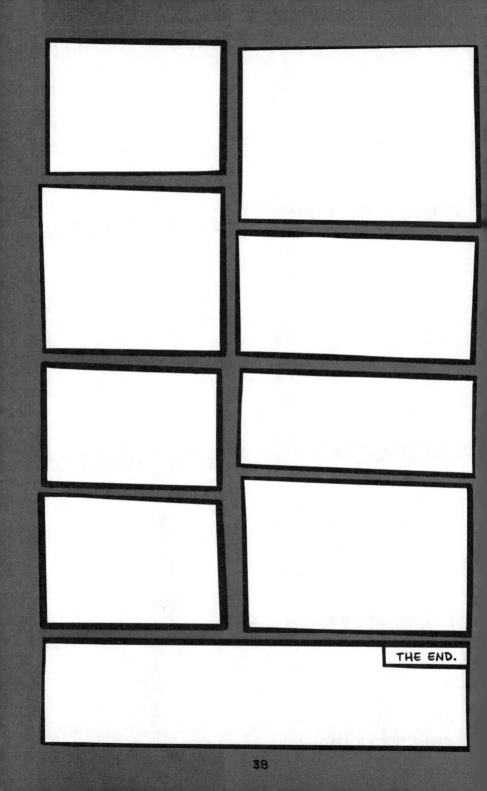

THE END.

CHARACTER EXAMPLES

(Feel free to use these guys, but
I suggest creating your own.)

GOOD GUYS . . .

Toast Man   Spatula Kid   Hammerhead

BAD GUYS . . .

Booger
Head

Stair
Master

Kitty
Litter

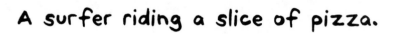

A surfer riding a slice of pizza.

RaNDoM ACTs of DRAW-NeSS!

A fish jumping out of its
bowl and into a toilet.

Draw the foods you don't like on the plates.

Hank will eat it all!

Now, fill up your friend
with your favorite foods.

GREAT JOB!

Thumbs UP!

Add some more thumbprint
creatures to these scenes.

Try giving
this thumbprint
creature more
alien friends!

47

A ballerina hippopotamus.

Here's mine.
Try tracing it as
fast as you can!

RaNDOM ACTs
oF DRAW-
NeSS!

ROBO-HAND!

1. Grab a crayon and trace your hand on the next page.

2. Make each finger a funky robot. (Give them antennae, lightbulbs, dials, buttons, etc.)

3. Good job! Now, color each robot.

BEEP
BOOP
o
BLIP

Draw a BEARD on these animals.
(Remember, they love colors.)

Newt

Unicorn

Turtle

Koala

Fly

Toucan

Snake

More animals with BEARDS . . .

Rhinoceros

Chicken

Pig

Platypus

squirrel

Giraffe

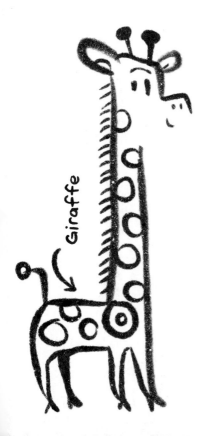

Rollie
pollie

Now draw an animal on these BEARDS!

More BEARDS
to add animals to.

Okay. Draw twenty lines from top to bottom on these two pages. Now draw twenty lines from one side to the other.

Great job! Now, using different colors,
fill in all those little squares!

Here's some more LINE art! ROUND TWO!

Take this line and turn it into a cat
reading a book on a surfboard.

Okay, you're doing awesomely, but now it gets a bit harder. With the line below, draw a unicorn jumping off a diving board into a swimming pool.

You're getting the hang of this!
Okay, using the line below, draw a monkey
wearing a cape, flying in the air, and
holding a walrus.

Fantastic work! Here's the last one. Using this line, draw a whale eating ice cream with an octopus on a warm, sunny day.

A wiener dog eating a
hot dog on a Ferris wheel.

DRAW WITH YOUR Foot!

(what?! That's WILD I know.)

Grab a pencil (or crayon) and trace the fish using only your foot.

An elephant climbing a cactus.

A unicorn with its horn
stuck in a tree.

Draw a silly hat and funny glasses on each of these faces . . .

Remember to try and make each hat and glasses different.

(Then color the whole page!! WOOHOO!!)

A bulldog juggling toilet paper.

WATCH OUT FOR THE FLYING TOILET PAPER!

RaNDoM AcTs of DRAW-Ness!

Using objects instead of actual letters, draw your name. (Just pick an object that begins with each letter in your name.)

Here's an example:

"B"
BAT

"R"
RAKE

"A"
ARMADILLO

"D"
DINOSAUR

"Y"
YO-YO

There's more room on the next page, too!

After you do your name, try
your family and friends' names, too!

A poodle Hula-Hooping.

Try something like
this. Have fun
making it your own!

RaNDoM ACTs
of DRAW-
Ness!

FREESTYLE

DOODLE LIKE CRAZY! HAVE FUN!

Can you guess the
page number without
flipping the page?
DRAW YOUR GUESS!

Animal Mash-Up!

Okay, I'll give you three different critters. Then you combine them and color them!

Here's an example:
A hammerhead shark, a duck, and a snail.

Don't forget to color it!

Okay, mash up a bear, a turtle,
and a bunny.

Don't forget to color it, too!

Now mash up a fish, a fly,
and a kangaroo!

color, color, color!

Mash up a dog, a cow, and a caterpillar.

wow! Awesome job!
Okay, now get to coloring. Yahoo!!

Mash up a bat, a walrus, and a newt.

Seriously, great job! Woo-hoo!!

A hedgehog on a scooter in front of the Eiffel Tower.

Random Acts of DRAW-Ness!

A triceratops playing tennis.

Trace this one and try to be speedy!

A llama in a tuxedo
playing a saxophone.

RaNDoM ACTs
of DRAW-
Ness!

A cat in space being chased
by a two-headed alien.

*PS You can put whatever you want inside, too!
A pickle, cheese, a lamp, even a dinosaur. Just
have fun, be super silly, and feel free to draw
outside the lines!

Draw your favorite part of your favorite movie or TV show!

A dolphin sitting on the moon having a milkshake.

Look in a mirror and draw yourself.

Great stuff! Last one, draw yourself
upside down. No cheating and flipping the
book around, either! Nice try! ☺

A woolly mammoth on a
hoverboard boxing a bear.

RANDOM ACTS
OF DRAW-
NESS!

This next super fun section is called . . .
FILL IT UP!
I've drawn stuff to fill up with your favorite things. Food, toys, pets, even sugary sweets. Woo-hoo!
INK

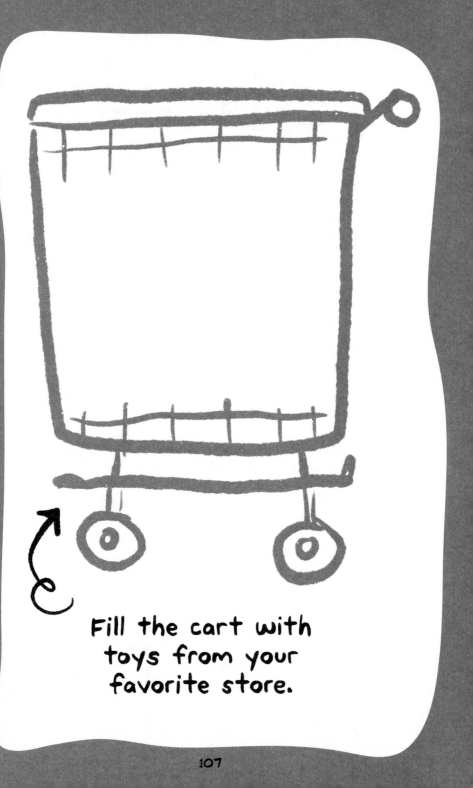

Fill the cart with
toys from your
favorite store.

Fill this pond with some fun animals, ducks, turtles, a whale!

Fill this aquarium with
some awesome pets!
Fish, lizards,
hamsters, whatever.

A monkey wearing a fedora
riding a motorcycle.

A shark scuba diving, eating a sandwich while taking a selfie.

RaNDoM ACTS of DRAW-NeSS!

A zombie football player.

How creepy is
this guy?!
Try making
yours scarier!

Draw twenty-five circles . . .
when you're done, give
each circle a face!

Like me

Bath time!
But wait! You forgot your tub toys. Better get to drawing. Be silly, please!

An astronaut riding a
longhorn bull in space.

An armadillo eating
nachos by the pool.

A blindfolded mermaid cooking dinner underwater.

The Future You!

Okay, on this next page, draw you as a grown-up! What do you want to be? An astronaut, a singer, a deep-sea diver, a unicorn trainer, a beekeeper, a chef, a professional juggler? Whatever it is, draw and then color it!

A polar bear wearing a top hat playing a violin.

RaNDoM ACTs of DRAW-Ness!

A flamingo in a tower throwing a pie in someone's face.